THE
PICNIC PROBLEM
(Maths)

Written by
Jonathan Litton

Illustrated by
Magalí Mansilla

Max and Suzy were playing at home.
An envelope dropped through the letterbox
and landed on the mat. "Read it out, Suzy!"
said Max with excitement.

Three, two, one,
it's time for fun,
a maths picnic awaits!
Head to the park,
where your first clue,
is waiting on the gates.

From
Miss Add-It-Up

"It sounds like a puzzle,"
said Suzy. "Let's go!"
And off they ran to the park.

They found the first clue pinned to the park gates. Max read it out:

Choose your route across the lake,
count seven stones, make no mistake!

They looked at the two paths of stepping stones.
"I know which path to take," said Max.
"So do I," said Suzy. "Let's count our way across."

Do you know which path
Suzy and Max should take?

"1, 2, 3, 4, 5, 6, 7!" they giggled,
as they skipped across the stepping stones.

"Look, there's the second clue!"
said Max, pointing to the tree trunk.

Look up high, you'll know you're right
When you spy a big, square kite!

"There are three kites," said
Suzy, "which one is the square?"

"I see it!" said Max. "The kite in the middle is a square on its side."

The woman flying the square kite was their maths teacher, Miss Add-It-Up! She reeled it in and tied to the tail was the third clue.

9

Which kite has the longest tail?
Ignore the strings, so you don't fail.

"That's a tricky puzzle!" said Suzy.
"The tails are tangled up!"

"Let's try and work it out!"
said Max. "Maybe the triangular
kite has the longest tail?"

The kite flyers switched positions and untangled their kites. The ribbons flowed freely.

"Look!" shouted Suzy. "The square kite has quite a long tail, the triangular kite has a longer tail, but the circular kite has the longest tail of all!"

Suzy was right. The circular kite did have the longest tail and tied to it was the fourth clue.

Three of us are flying kites,
while two are solving clues.
Three plus two is how many?
Which number will you choose?

Max answered, "Three plus two is FIVE!"
Suzy added, "The roundabout has five
seats – I wonder if that's where we'll
find the next clue?"

Max found the fifth clue on the
roundabout and read it aloud:

The final challenge, before you eat,
is to add up all your feet.

"We each have two feet," said Suzy.
"Let's count them all up in twos."
She pointed at her feet and shouted, "I have two!"
Max shouted out, "And mine make four!"

"Six, eight, TEN!" they each called out in turn.

"Ten is the correct answer. Well done!" said Miss Add-It-Up, and she spread out a picnic rug in a sunny spot.

"Can you use your number skills to solve the sandwich puzzle?" she asked.

"I have ten sandwiches to divide between five people. If each person has the same number of sandwiches, how many will each person have?"

"TWO SANDWICHES EACH!"

Max and Suzy answered together.

"That's right!" said Miss Add-It-Up, as she handed out the sandwiches two at a time, counting, "2, 4, 6, 8, 10."

YUM, YUM!
Everyone tucked into their picnic...

...but the best was yet to come!

Miss Add-It-Up surprised them all with an apple pie, which she divided into five equal slices – one each!

WELL DONE MAX AND SUZY!

Miss Add-It-Up served Max and Suzy first, and everyone cheered the two little mathematicians!

Let's talk about maths!

The maths behind the story

Let's look at the problems Suzy and Max faced in the story. Turn to the page numbers for help, or find the answers on the next page.

p.5

p.6

Addition and subtraction

Addition is when you find the total of two or more numbers. Subtraction is when you take one or more numbers away from another.

Suzy and Max counted 7 stones in one path and 5 stones in the other. How many stones were there altogether?

How many more stones were there in the first path than the second?

Your turn

We add and subtract every day, for example when we pay and receive change at the shops. If you have 10p and you are given 5p, how much money do you have?

p.8

Shapes and names

Objects have a shape or form, like a circle-shaped wheel or a rectangle-shaped door.

Can you name these four shapes?

Your turn

Can you find examples of these shapes in your home? What other shapes can you find and name?

p.17

p.21

Multiplication and division

Multiplication is adding in equal groups. Division is when you share objects into equal groups.

If Miss Add-It-Up divides her pie into 10 slices, how many slices will each person receive?

If Miss Add-It-Up shares 15 sandwiches equally, how many will everyone have?

Your turn

Now try this multiplication question: if you buy 4 bunches of bananas, with 5 bananas in each bunch, how many bananas will you buy altogether?

Answers

If you need help finding the answers, try reading the page again.

Addition and subtraction: There are 12 stepping stones in total.
7 + 5 = 12.
There are two more stones in the top path than the bottom.
7 - 5 = 2.
Your turn: 10p + 5p = 15p

Shapes and names: The shapes are a triangle, square, circle and rectangle.

Multiplication and division: Miss Add-It-Up gives everyone 2 slices of pie. 10 ÷ 5 = 2. Then she shares 15 sandwiches equally between 5 people, so everyone has 3 sandwiches. 15 ÷ 5 = 3.
Your turn: 20 bananas. 4 x 5 = 20.

Quarto is the authority on a wide range of topics.

Quarto educates, entertains and enriches the lives of our readers—enthusiasts and lovers of hands-on living.

www.quartoknows.com

Author: Jonathan Litton
Illustrator: Magalí Mansilla
Consultant: Ed Walsh
Editors: Jacqueline McCann,
 Carly Madden, Ellie Brough
Designer: Sarah Chapman-Suire

© 2018 Quarto Publishing plc

First published in 2018 by QED Publishing, an imprint of The Quarto Group. The Old Brewery, 6 Blundell Street, London, N7 9BH, United Kingdom. T (0)20 7700 6700 F (0)20 7700 8066 www.QuartoKnows.com

A catalogue record for this book is available from the British Library.

ISBN 978-0-71123-987-6

9 8 7 6 5 4 3 2 1

Manufactured in Dongguan, China
TL062018

FSC
MIX
Paper from responsible sources
FSC® C104723
www.fsc.org

Find out more...

Here are links to websites where you will find more information on maths.

BBC Bitesize
www.bbc.co.uk/bitesize/ks1/maths

Topmarks
www.topmarks.co.uk/maths-games/5-7-years/counting

CHILDREN SHOULD BE SUPERVISED WHEN USING THE INTERNET, PARTICULARLY WHEN USING AN UNFAMILIAR WEBSITE FOR THE FIRST TIME. THE PUBLISHERS AND AUTHOR CANNOT BE HELD RESPONSIBLE FOR THE CONTENT OF THE WEBSITES REFERRED TO IN THIS BOOK.